How to Be a Dragon

Written by
Anne Rooney

Illustrated by
Andy Hamilton

Published in 2026 by
Norwood House Press
2544 Clinton Street
Buffalo, NY 14224

Printed in the United States of America

Library of Congress Cataloging-in-Publication Data:
Names: Rooney, Anne, author. | Hawkins, Daisy, author. | Hamilton, Andy, illustrator. | Serafin, Miriam, illustrator.
Title: How to be a dragon / written by Anne Rooney, illustrated by Andy Hamilton. Pushing Sophie / written by Daisy Hawkins, illustrated by Miriam Serafin.
Description: Buffalo, NY : Norwood House Press, 2026. | Series: Phonics all-stars: phase 5c
Identifiers: ISBN 9781978578296 (pbk.) | ISBN 9781978578302 (library bound) | ISBN 9781978578319 (ebook)
Subjects: LCSH: Reading–Phonetic method–Juvenile literature. | English language–Phonetics–Juvenile literature. | Dragons–Juvenile fiction. | Computer programming–Juvenile fiction.
Classification: LCC LB1573.3 R665 2026 | DDC 372.465–dc23

CPSIA compliance information: Batch #CW26NHP: For further information contact Norwood House Press at 1-800-237-9932.

Dragon

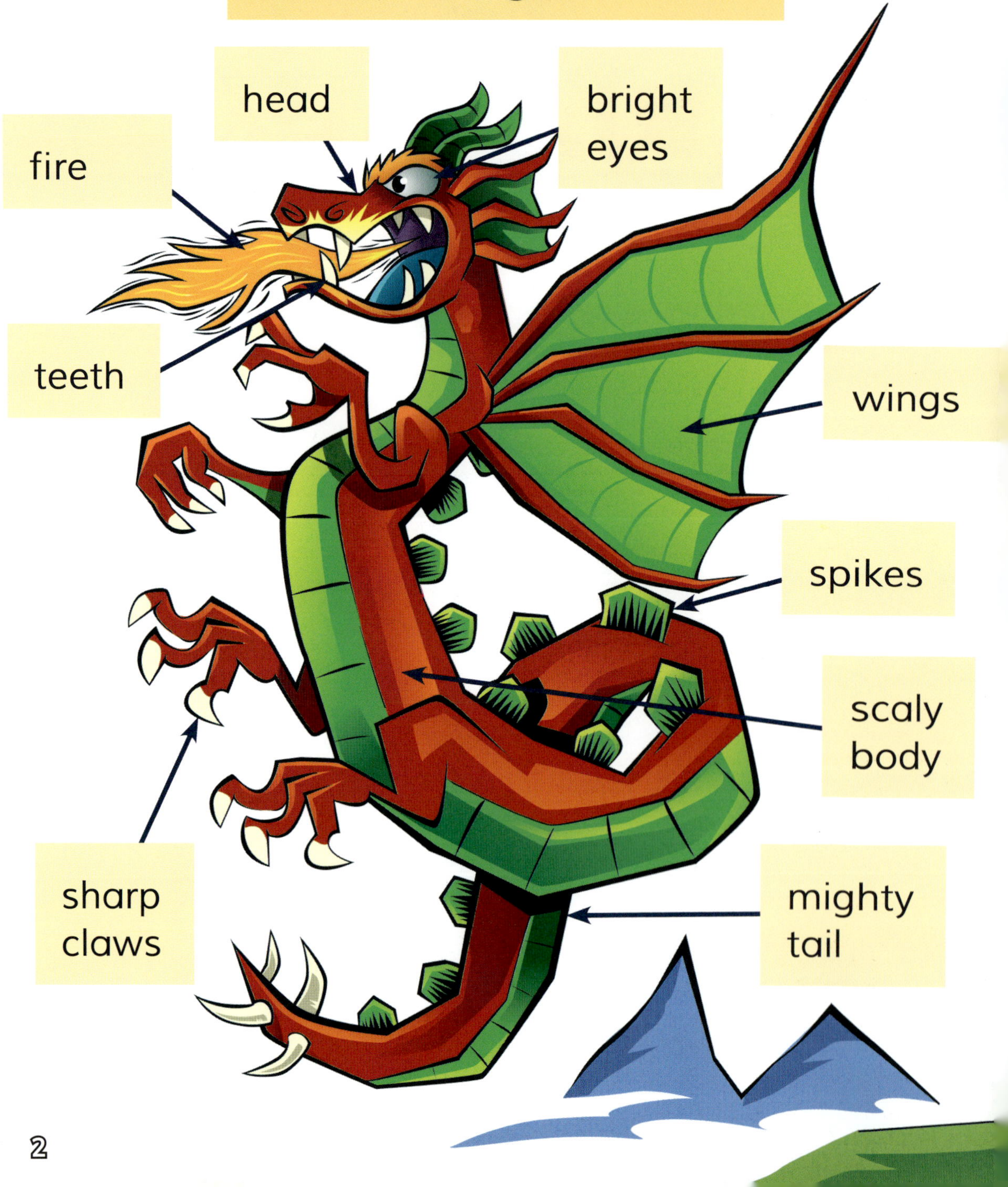
head
bright eyes
fire
teeth
wings
spikes
scaly body
sharp claws
mighty tail

Knight

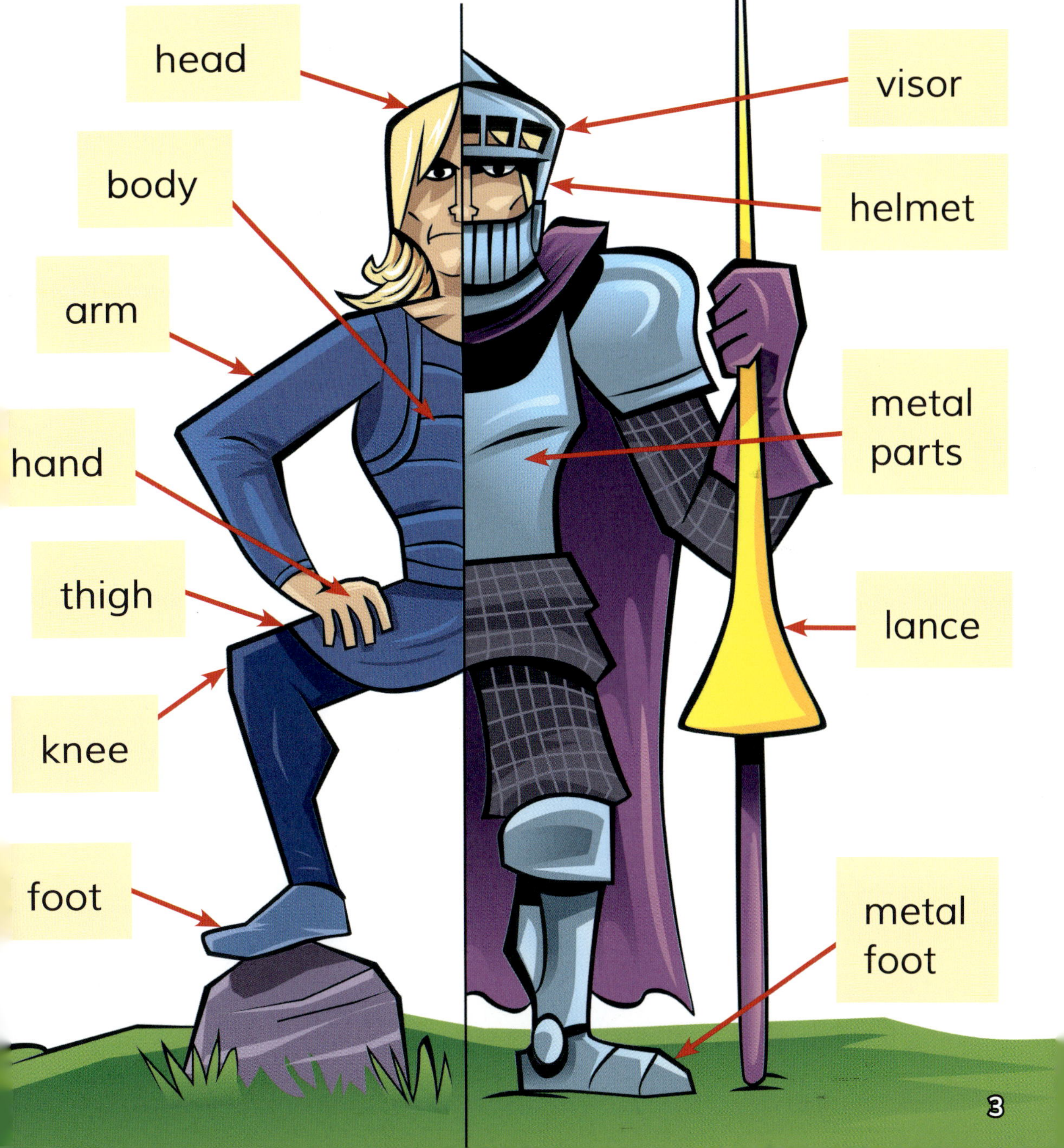
head
body
arm
hand
thigh
knee
foot
visor
helmet
metal parts
lance
metal foot

So you are a dragon. That means that you need a cave to live in.

The best cave is high in a mountain that is difficult for people to climb. It must have a wide landing place right outside, so you can take flight quickly and land easily.

The cave should go deep inside the rock.

You need space to stockpile your treasure, somewhere to hide a princess, and a place to lie and sleep.

A dragon is a wily predator. You should not need to roam the forests hunting food.

Your dinner should come to you.

First, you need to capture a princess.

You will not eat a princess. You will eat knights.

But you need a princess to lure knights.

Where to find a princess

on the road

in an oak forest

by a frog and
toad pond

on a carnival float

Keep your captured princess in a light part of the cave, by the entrance. If a knight can see her, or hear her singing or sighing, he will try to rescue her. He will start a fight.

Knights have a metal outside. Do not use too much fire. The metal will melt and spoil the flavor of the knight.

Do not eat the metal parts. You must peel the knight first. (You can add the metal parts to your treasure pile.)

You can eat the horse if you are still hungry.

All dragons collect treasure.

You will not eat gold and jewels. You will eat people who come to steal your bright, shiny treasure.

Pile your treasure high. Leave one trinket in sight beside the entrance. A knight or villager might spy it.

Hide behind your treasure. If you do it right, a knight or villager will come to steal some, and you can leap out.

At night, your treasure will gleam in the moonlight. Sleep with one eye open, ready to pounce.

Treasure has lots of uses. It delights princesses too. They will not try to escape if you have loads of treasure.

When you have an egg, you can use treasure to hide it.

People do not like dragons. They will try to destroy your egg if they find it, so put it out of sight behind your treasure.

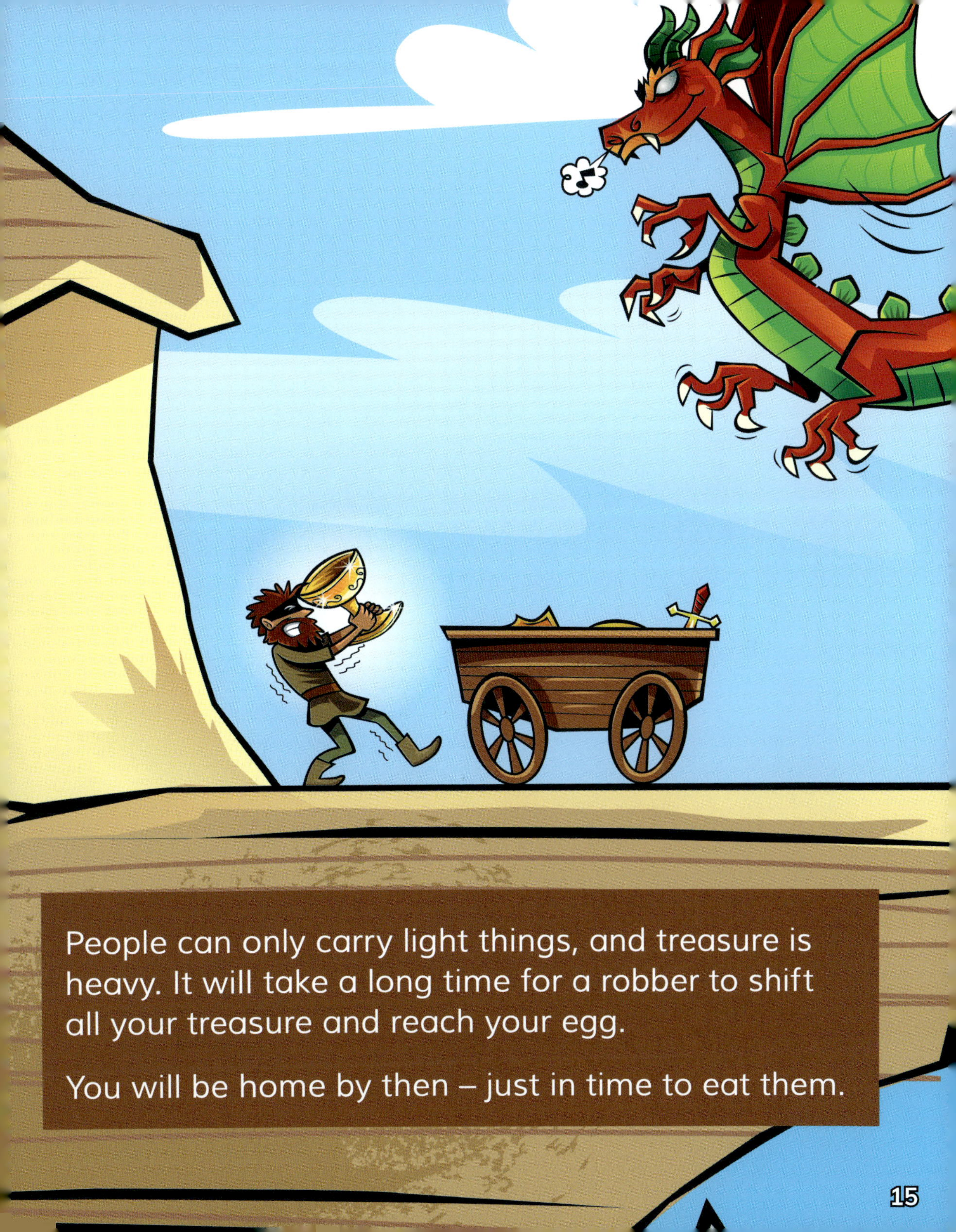

People can only carry light things, and treasure is heavy. It will take a long time for a robber to shift all your treasure and reach your egg.

You will be home by then – just in time to eat them.

When your egg hatches, teach your tiny dragon the lessons you have learned.

Pushing Sophie

Written by
Daisy Hawkins

Illustrated by
Miriam Serafin

Sophie had been playing the clarinet since she was three years old.

"There is no music like clarinet music," Sophie's mom would say, as she made Sophie practice day after day, year after year.

Sophie did not agree. She found the clarinet so boring!

But she knew it made her mom happy.

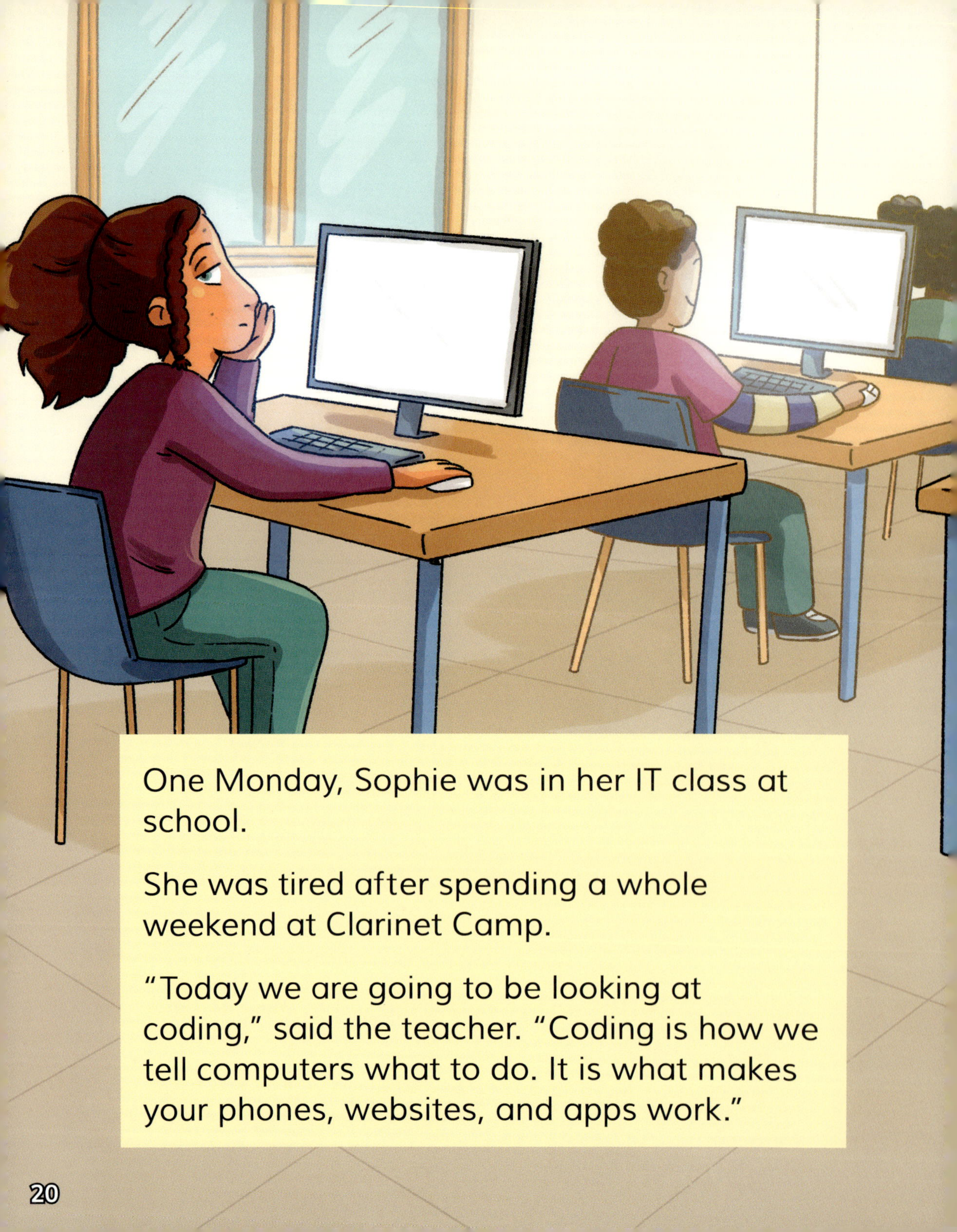

One Monday, Sophie was in her IT class at school.

She was tired after spending a whole weekend at Clarinet Camp.

"Today we are going to be looking at coding," said the teacher. "Coding is how we tell computers what to do. It is what makes your phones, websites, and apps work."

Sophie sat up in her seat, instantly captivated.

In the lesson, Sophie picked up the basics of coding really quickly.

Soon, she was better than anyone else.

Scanning computer code was a bit like reading sheet music.

Plus, playing the clarinet had given her fast fingers for typing.

From then on, when Sophie was at home, she did as her mom asked – at least in the daytime.

"Clean your clarinet," her mom told her. Then, "Practice, practice, practice."

Then, at night, Sophie would sit in her room and write code.

She even learned how to compile software.

One night, her mom crept into Sophie's room and spied on her daughter.

"Sophie! What are you doing? It is so late – you will be too tired for clarinet tomorrow."

"Not everything is about the clarinet," Sophie snapped.

Then her lip started to quiver. She had not meant to snap at her mom.

“Don’t you love the clarinet?” her mom asked.

“I love that playing the clarinet makes you happy,” said Sophie.

Shocked, Sophie’s mom sat down next to her.

“You make me happy, Sophie, whether you play the clarinet or not,” her mom told her. “I’m sorry I got so caught up in it. I wanted to play it myself as a child, but I could never get the hang of it.”

Sophie felt her mom's eyes drift to the computer screen.

"It's code," Sophie giggled. Then she started to explain.

Her mom listened intently, full of praise for how much Sophie knew.

"You know, the first computer programmer was Ada Lovelace," said Sophie. "That was over a hundred years ago. It was her mom who supported her – who believed in her."

“Just sometimes, you have to let children be who they are,” said Sophie softly.

At that, Sophie and her mom gave each other a big hug. They both knew that, from now on, things would be different.